I0505757

Ruby Programming
Professional Made Easy
By Sam Key

Expert Ruby Programming
Language Success in a Day for
any Computer User
2nd *Edition*

Copyright 2015 by Sam Key - All rights reserved.

In no way is it legal to reproduce, duplicate, or transmit any part of this document in either electronic means or in printed format. Recording of this publication is strictly prohibited and any storage of this document is not allowed unless with written permission from the publisher. All rights reserved.

Table Of Contents

Introduction

I want to thank you and congratulate you for purchasing the book, *"Professional Ruby Programming Made Easy: Expert Ruby Programming Language Success in a Day for Any Computer User!"*

This book contains proven steps and strategies on how to write basic lines of code in Ruby. This is especially made for amateur programmers with little to no experience in coding.

Ruby is a programming language which people think is ideal for newbies in the programming field. Congratulations on choosing this programming language. In this book, you will be introduced to all the fundamental aspects of coding in Ruby.

This book will give you a huge boost in your programming skills. However, it is also important to quickly supplement yourself with advanced Ruby tutorials after you are done with this book to retain the knowledge you gain from it.

Thanks again for purchasing this book, I hope you enjoy it!

Chapter 1: Setting Up

This book will assume that you are a bit familiar with computer programming and have made a few lines of codes in some programming languages. However, it does not mean that you cannot Ruby unless you have no idea about programming languages.

Unfortunately, a person with a little bit of experience in computer programming might even encounter difficulties in learning this programming language. One of the reasons that might cause that is the difference between Ruby and other languages.

Most programming languages are almost alike. It is even safe to say that the only difference between those programs is the keywords or commands in their arsenals. Ruby on the other hand, is similar but offer new concepts or fairly new methods to programming and coding.

In layman terms, learning Ruby will require you to learn a different 'programming culture'. Nevertheless, you do not need to think about it too much. In the end, whatever language you will use, you still only have one goal. And that goal is to create programs.

Just a Simple Note

From time to time, the book will provide further explanation of terms and methods that can easily confuse new programmers. In case you encounter a foreign term in the discussion, just take note of it since it and other such terms will be discussed later.

In addition, be always ready to explore the web. Even though the book is comprehensive when it comes to basic topics, you will still be put to some situations that the book will not be able to help you achieve the things you want to happen in your program. Many websites on the net can provide you answers during those times. Take advantage of that fact.

Getting Ruby

Before anything else, get the latest stable version of Ruby from the web. As of this writing, Ruby's stable version is 2.1.5.

Go to https://www.ruby-lang.org/en/documentation/installation/. In there, you can get the right installer package for the operating system that your computer is running on.

Be mindful of what you are going to download. Many people tend to download the source code of Ruby instead of the installation packages. Also, you must make sure that the installation package you will get is suited for your computer's operating system. You would not want to get a Mac version of the language when your computer is running on Microsoft Windows.

Installation of Ruby is not that difficult. Just open the installer, and the setup will provide you with step-by-step instructions. While you are installing Ruby, take note of the location or directory where you will install it. Once you are done with the installation, open Ruby's interactive shell.

Note for Windows Users

For people who are using a computer running on Windows, you will find the interactive interpreter inside the bin folder located inside your Ruby installation folder. The file is named irb.bat. If you have installed Ruby using the default location, the interactive shell will be located at: "c:\Ruby21\bin\irb.bat".

On the other hand, if you are using Windows 7 or higher, you can just open the interactive shell using the search box on the Windows menu. Open the menu, and type in Ruby. Commonly, the Windows menu will provide you two results — ruby.exe and Interactive Ruby. Choose the latter.

What is the interactive shell anyway? In Ruby, you can program using two modes: the interactive mode and the programming mode.

Ruby's Interactive Mode

The interactive mode or IRB (Interactive Ruby Shell) is an environment wherein Ruby will provide immediate feedback in every line of code or statement you type in to it. It is an ideal environment where new Ruby programmers can test and experiment with codes quickly. You will be using this mode in most parts of this book.

Probably, you will stick on it most of the time. However, a few might want to use the programming mode instead. You can use which one you like, but if you have no idea about which one to use, stick with the interactive mode.

The interactive mode or shell will appear like a typical console or command prompt. In the shell, you should be familiar with two things. First is the cursor. Second is the prompt.

The cursor indicates where you can type or if you can type anything. In the interpreter shell, you can use overtype mode on this by pressing the insert key on your keyboard. You can return to insert mode by pressing the insert key again.

The prompt will look like this: irb(main):001:0>. If this prompt is on, it means that Ruby is ready to accept a line of code or statement from you. For now, type a letter a in the prompt and press the Enter key. The shell or interpreter will move the cursor, show a bunch of text, and display the prompt once again:

```
irb(main):001:0> a
NameError:  undefined   local   variable   or
method 'a' for main:Object
     from (irb):1
     from C:/Ruby21/bin/irb:11:in '<main>'
irb(main):002:0>
```

This time, type "a" on the shell and then press the Enter key. Instead of an error, you have received => "a". Now, type "1" without the quotes. Just like before, the interpreter just provided you with a reply containing the number you entered.

Why does the letter a without the quotes returned an error? As you can see, Ruby provided you with an error message when you just entered the letter a without quotes. In Ruby, characters enclosed in double or single quotes are treated differently.

In the case of the letter a, Ruby understood that when you input "a" with the quotes, you meant that you are inputting the letter a. On the other hand, Ruby thought of something else when you input the letter a without the quotes, which will be discussed later.

You will receive error messages like the one before or other variations of it if you input something that violates Ruby's syntax or something that is impossible to be evaluated or executed by the interpreter. In simple terms, Ruby will provide you notifications like that if it does not understand what you said or cannot do what you commanded.

Now, type "1 + 1", without the double quotes, and press the Enter key. Instead of an error, you will receive this instead:

=> 2

Every time you press the Enter key, the shell check the command or statement you created. If it does not violate the syntax, it will proceed on checking if every word and symbols you placed make sense. Once the statement passes that check, it will evaluate and execute the statement and provide a result or feedback.

In this case, Ruby has evaluated the addition operation you commanded and replied the number 2, which is the sum of 1 + 1. Just before the number 2, an equal sign and "greater than" sign were placed. Those two denotes that the next value is the result of the statement you entered.

You might have thought that Ruby can be a good calculator. Indeed it is, but statements like "1 + 1" and "a" are only processed like that in the interactive mode of Ruby. If you include a line like that when coding in programming mode, you will certainly encounter a syntax error.

Ruby's Programming Mode
On the other hand, the programming mode is a method wherein you can execute blocks of code in one go. You will need to type the code of your program first before you can run and see what it will do.

You will need a text editor to type your program. Any simple text editor such as Notepad in Windows is sufficient for programming Ruby. However, to reduce typos and keyword mistakes, it is advisable that you use a source code editor, which will provide you with syntax highlighting and checking. In Windows users, a few of the best source code editors you can use for Ruby programming are Notepad++, TextWrangler, JEdit, and Crimson Editor.

Once you are done typing your code, save it as a .rb file. For Windows users: if you have let Ruby associate .rb and .rbw files to it, all .rb files or Ruby code you have created can be opened by just double clicking on them. They will act as if they are typical Windows program.

By the way, programming mode does not provide instant reply to your expressions. For example, if you input a = 1 + 1 in interactive mode, it will reply with => 2. In programming mode, that statement will not provide any output.

Also, if one of the lines encounters an error, the program will stop executing the next lines after the line that generated the error.

Using Both at the Same Time (and Some IRB tricks)

Yes, you can use the same mode at the same time. You can just simply type in the code that you want to run later in a source code editor. If you want to test run the code, you will need to copy everything that you have written and paste it on the Interactive Ruby Shell.

How can you do that? You can actually right click on the shell and click on the Paste option on the context menu that will appear. However, take note that the keyboard shortcut Ctrl+V does not work in the Interactive Ruby Shell.

When you paste code in the Interactive Ruby Shell, it will process the code as if you type them individually on the shell. Every line break that is present on your code will be treated as if you pressed the enter key while coding in the shell. That's where the advantage in using both mode at the same time.

Since the Interactive Ruby Shell will accept your pasted code one time at a time, it will provide you will immediate feedback on your code. It could be messy at first, but it is an effective method to debug your code, which will be helpful later in your Ruby programming days.

There is a bit of a downside in doing this though. The Interactive Ruby Shell will retain all the instructions and data you gave it. It might cause a bit of a problem if you try to use it twice on the same code. A quick fix to that is to close the console. And open another one.

On the other hand, you can also copy the blocks of text that you made in the Interactive Ruby Shell. To do that, right click on the window and choose the mark option. You can mark the text that you want to copy from the Interactive Ruby Shell.

However, do note that the marking or selecting the text from the shell is different from marking or selecting text on your browser or text editor. The marker works by selecting all the text within the 'box' that you highlight and it will not automatically highlight line by line. In order to copy the line that you marked, right click on the interactive window.

And if ever you want to find something that you have typed or a message the interactive console replied, you can just right click and click on the Find option in the context menu.

Lastly, if you get stuck somewhere in your code and you cannot go forward in the Interactive Ruby Shell, you can just press Ctrl+C to get out from whatever you are doing. That method is much easier than closing the interactive shell and losing all the things that you have typed.

Chapter 2: Programming Basics

Before you dive into the world of Ruby, you must prep yourself with some programming basics. In this chapter, you will be introduced in the fundamental concepts of programming.

Knowing the basics of programming is essential if you are a beginner. If you are experienced with programming, you can skip this part. Though, it might be a good idea to give this chapter a read. You might gain new ideas that you are unfamiliar.

Computer Program

First of all, what is a computer program? A program is just a file that contains instructions that the computer must do in order to achieve the program's purpose.

Open your computer's calculator program. It is a good example of a program that you can actually do in Ruby. If you are going to create a program like a calculator, you must write instructions like the ones below in order for your computer to allow you to compute using a calculator.

- Create a window for the calculator program

- Place some buttons on the window for the user to press and input numbers or operations

- Place a text box where the user can keep track of the equations that he inputted

- Wait for the user to press a button and input a number

- Accept the number and wait for the user to press a button for an operator

- Wait for the user to press a button and input the next number

- Repeat the previous processes until the user press the equal sign button

- Calculate the numbers and perform the necessary information

- Update the text box and show the answer to the equation

- Wait again for the user to do something

- If the user presses the x button, close the program

Programming Language

Of course, programming is not as simple as that. You cannot just tell the computer what to do. And that is the reason you will need to use a programming language like Ruby.

Computers cannot understand English, but they can understand programming languages as well. But take note that not all computers can understand all languages. For example, a program built in a different language for a smartphone cannot be easily executed in a computer. That is also the reason Mac or Linux computers cannot run programs for Windows.

Anyway, learning a programming language is like learning human language. And to be honest, learning a programming language is much easier than a dialect. That is true. It is safe to say that human language is more complex than a programming language.

For example, the word print in English can mean a lot of things. In Ruby, the word or keyword print means that the computer needs to print something on the screen.

On the other hand, learning one programming language can let you learn other programming languages easier. Most of them has the same quirks, same rules, but offers different limitations.

With newer programming languages, a programmer does not need to learn all of them. If you look at the big picture, they are all the same. And choosing which is best or better boils down to your preferences.

Learning Ruby does not mean you need to learn Python, Java, or Lua. Also, you can live by without learning the old ones like C++, Ada, or even Pascal. But of course, it is recommendable that you explore and take a look at them. After all, you cannot really determine your preferences if you will just stick to one programming language. Also, checking them out will make you understand program development better.

Moving forward, just like human language, programming language follow a set of 'grammar rules' called syntax. Once you get the hang of the syntax rules in a programming language, you can pretty much do a lot in programming. And fortunately, you can learn the basic syntax of Ruby in a day. Ruby's syntax will be discussed on the next chapter.

Being a Program Developer or Programmer

To become a programmer, you do not need to be a Math whiz. As long as you have sound knowledge when it comes to College Algebra and Logic, you will fare well in creating programs.

On the other hand, you must have a lot of patience and you must be attentive to details. Unlike other jobs, programming involves a lot of trial and error — at first. Also, you must be capable of working smart. In programming, having a 'reinventing the wheel' attitude will only hinder your growth. Recreating your own version of a function instead of imitating one that has been created by another will only waste your time. Instead, it is much better for you to 'improve the wheel' or improve and understand the function or code that you will acquire.

With all of that said, it is now time to embark on learning Ruby.

Chapter 3: Ruby Syntax

In the first chapter, you have encountered your first syntax error. For those who are not familiar with the term syntax (or forgotten what you have learned in the previous chapter), syntax is a set of 'language' rules that you must follow in order for a programming language (in this case, Ruby) to understand you.

A programming language's syntax is similar to English grammar where you need to correctly arrange parts of the sentence—such as verbs, nouns, and adjectives—to make it coherent and grammatically correct.

The two major differences between Ruby's syntax (or other programming languages' syntax as well) and English's set of grammar rules are Ruby's syntax's strictness and inflexibility. It is set to behave like that because computers, unlike humans, cannot understand or comprehend context. Also, if computers understand context and programming languages' syntaxes become lax, computer programming will become difficult.

First, computer will become prone to misunderstanding or misinterpreting your statements. If you point to a jar of jam in a shelf full of jars and requested people to get the one you want, most of them will surely get and give you the wrong jar. That kind of situation will happen if a programming language's syntax became too loose or forgiving.

Here are some of Ruby's syntax rules:

Whitespace

Whitespace (continuous spaces and tabs) are ignored in Ruby code unless they are placed inside strings. For example, the expression "1 + 1", "1 + 1", or 1+1 will provide the same result in Ruby. On the other hand, if the space is within a string or enclosed inside quotation marks, then the whitespace character will not be ignored.

```
irb(main):046:0> 1  + 1
=> 2
irb(main):047:0> 1 +              1
=> 2
irb(main):048:0> 1+1
=> 2
irb(main):049:0>
```

Line Ending Terminators

New lines and semicolons are treated as line endings. Ruby works by reading your program's lines one by one. Each line is considered a statement. A statement is a combination of keywords, operators, values, methods, and properties, which is translated as a command.

Every time you put a semicolon or move to the next line, the previous line will be treated as a statement. There are some cases that if you do not place a semicolon but used a new line character (the one that the Enter key produces and pushes the cursor to move to the next line) to write a new line of code will make Ruby think that the previous line and the new line of code is just one statement. For example:

```
irb(main):042:0> 1 + 1
=> 2
irb(main):043:0> 1 +
irb(main):044:0* 1 +
irb(main):045:0* 1
=> 4
```

If you typed that in Ruby's interactive mode, you will not encounter an error or reply from Ruby. Instead, it allowed you to move on to the next line and type another line of code.

If you have noticed, the greater than sign at the end of the prompt changed into an asterisk. The asterisk denotes that all the succeeding lines of code after the previous one will be treated as one statement in Ruby or the next lines are meant to be continuations of the previous line.

Ruby behaved like that since you left an operator at the end of the line and did not place a value on the operator's right hand side. So, Ruby is treating the example as 1 + 1 +. If you place another 1 at the last line, Ruby will interpret that 1 as the last value to your expression and evaluate it. It will then produce a reply, which is => 3.

Case Sensitivity

Identifiers or names of constants, variables, and methods in Ruby are case sensitive. For example, a variable named vAriable1 is different from variable1:

```
irb(main):040:0> vAriable1 = 2
=> 2
irb(main):041:0> variable1
NameError: undefined local variable or
method `variable1' for main:Object
        from (irb):41
        from C:/Ruby22/bin/irb:11:in
`<main>'
irb(main):042:0>
```

Aside from an undefined error, carelessly using capital letters at the start of your variables might lead you to defining a constant instead. Constants will be discussed later.

Comments

In computer languages, comments are used to serve as markers, reminders, or explanations within the program. Comments are ignored by Ruby and are not executed like regular statements.

Some convert statements in order to disable them. It is handy during debugging or testing alternate statements to get what they want since deleting a statement may make them forget it after a few minutes of coding another line.

To create comments in Ruby, use the hash sign (#) to let Ruby know that the succeeding characters is a comment line. You can insert comments at the end of statements. For example:

```
irb(main):001:0> #This is a comment.
irb(main):002:0* 1 + 1
=> 2
irb(main):003:0> 1 + 1 #This is a comment.
=> 2
irb(main):003:0>
```

As you can see, the line after the hash sign was just ignored and Ruby just evaluated the expression 1 + 1.

In case you are going to start programming using Ruby's programming mode, there will be times that you will want to create multiple lines of comments. You can still use hash signs to create multiple lines. For example:

```
#This is a comment.
#This is another comment.
#This is the last comment.
```

If you do not want to use that method, you can do this by using the =begin and =end keyword. Below is an example on how to use them:

```
=begin
This is a comment
This is another comment.
This is the last comment.
=end
```

All lines after the =begin and before the =end keyword will be treated as comment lines.

Those are just the primary rules in Ruby's syntax. Some commands have syntax of their own. They will be discussed together with the commands themselves.

Chapter 4: Parts of a Statement

You have been seeing the term statement in the previous chapters. As mentioned before, a statement is a combination of keywords, operators, variables, constants, values, expressions, methods, and properties, which is translated as a command.

In this chapter, you will know what six of those parts are: variables, constants, keywords, values, operators, and expressions. Let's start with variables.

Variables

In Math, you know that variables are placeholders for values. For example:

```
x = 1 + 1
x = 2
y = 3
```

In the previous line, variable x has a value of 2 and variable y has a value of 3. Variables in Ruby (or other programming languages) act the same way – as placeholders. However, unlike in Math, variables in Ruby do not act as placeholders for numbers alone. It can contain different types of values like strings and objects.

To create variables in Ruby, all you need is to assign a value to one. For example:

```
irb(main):001:0> a = 12
```

That example commands Ruby to create a variable named a and assign the number 12 as its value. To check the value of a variable in Ruby's interpreter mode, input a on a new line and press the Enter key. It will produce the result:

```
irb(main):001:0> a
=> 12
```

A while ago, instead of getting a reply like that from Ruby, you receive this instead:

```
NameError: undefined local variable or
method 'a' for main:Object
    from (irb):1
    from C:/Ruby21/bin/irb:11:in '<main>'
```

Technically, the error means that Ruby was not able to find a variable or method with the name a. Now, when you input a, it does not produce that error anymore since you have already created a variable named a.

By the way, in computer programming, the names you give to variables and other entities in the program are called identifiers. Some call them IDs or tokens instead.

There are some set of rules when giving an identifier to a variable. Identifiers can contain letters, numbers, and underscores. A variable identifier must start with a lower case letter or an underscore. It may also contain one or more characters. Also, variable identifiers should not be the same with a keyword or reserved words.

Just like any programming languages, reserved or special keywords cannot be used as identifiers.

Take note that the last assignment statement will override the previous assignment when assigning values to variables. For example:

```
irb(main):001:0> a = 13
=> 13
irb(main):002:0> a = 1
=> 1
irb(main):003:0> a
=> 1
```

Constants

Constants are like variables, but you can only assign a value to them once in your program and their identifiers must start with an uppercase letter. Reassigning a value to them will generate an error or a warning. For example:

```
irb(main):032:0> Constant = 1
=> 1
irb(main):033:0> Constant = 12
(irb):33: warning: already initialized
constant Constant
(irb):32: warning: previous definition of
Constant was here
=> 12
irb(main):034:0> Constant
=> 12
irb(main):035:0>
```

Keywords

Keywords are special reserved words in Ruby that perform specific functions and commands. Some of them are placeholder for special values such as true, false, and nil.

You cannot use keywords as identifiers. If you do, you will get an error message. For example:

```
irb(main):035:0> nil = 123
SyntaxError: (irb):35: Can't assign to nil
```

```
nil = 123
     ^
        from C:/Ruby22/bin/irb:11:in
`<main>'
irb(main):036:0>
```

By the way, the nil value means that the entity that contains it does not have a value. To put it simply, all variables will have the nil value if no value was assigned to it. When they are used and they have nil as their value, Ruby will return a warning if the –w is on.

Values

In Ruby, there are multiple types of values that you can assign in a variable. In programming, they are called literals. In coding Ruby, you will be dealing with these literals every time.

Integers

You can write integers in four forms or numeral systems: decimal, hexadecimal, octal, and binary. To make Ruby understand that you are declaring integers in hexadecimal (base 16), octal (base 8), or binary (base 2), you should use prefixes or leading signs.

If you are going to use octal, use 0 (zero).

```
irb(main):052:0> 010
=> 8
```

If you are going to use hexadecimal, use 0x (zero-x).

```
irb(main):053:0> 0x10
=> 16
```

If you are going to use binary, use 0b (zero-b).

24

```
irb(main):054:0> 0b10
=> 2
```

If you are going to use decimal, there is no need for any optional leading signs.

```
irb(main):055:0> 10
=> 10
```

Depending on the size of the integer, it can be categorized in the class Fixnum or Bignum.

Floating Numbers

Any integer with decimals is considered a floating number. All floating numbers are under the class Float.

Strings

Strings are values inside single or double quotation marks. They are treated as text in Ruby. You can place expression evaluation inside strings without terminating your quotes. You can just insert expressions by using the hash sign and enclosing the expression using curly braces. For example:

```
irb(main):001:0> a = "the sum of 3 and 1 is:
#{3 + 1}."
=> "the sum of 3 and 1 is: 4."
```

You can also access variables or constants in Ruby and include them in a string by placing a hash sign (#) before the variable or constant's name. For example:

```
irb(main):001:0> b = "string inside
variable."
=> "string inside variable."
irb(main):002:0> b = "You can access a #{b}"
```

```
=> "You can access a string inside
variable."
```

Arrays

An array is a data type that can contain multiple data or values. Creating arrays in Ruby is simple. Type Array and then follow it with values enclosed inside square brackets. Make sure that you separate each value with a comma. Any exceeding commas will be ignored and will not generate error. For example:

```
irb(main):001:0> arraysample = Array[1, 2,
3]
=> [1, 2, 3]
```

To access a value of an array, you must use its index. The index of an array value depends on its location in the array. For example, the value 2 in the arraysample variable has an index number of 0. The value 2, has an index of 1. And the value 3, has an index of 2. The index increments by 1 and starts with zero.

Below is an example on how to access a value in an array:

```
irb(main):001:0> arraysample[2]
=> 3
```

Hashes or Associative Arrays:

Hashes are arrays that contain paired keys (named index) and values. Instead of a numbered index, you can assign and use keys to access your array values.

```
irb(main):001:0> hashsample = Hash["First"
=> 1, "Second" = > 2]
=> {"First"=>1, "Second"=>2]
```

To access a hash value, you just need to call it using its key instead of an index number. For example:

```
irb(main):001:0> hashsample["Second"]
=> 2
```

Expressions

Expressions are combinations of operators, variables, values, and/or keywords. Expressions result into a value or can be evaluated by Ruby. A good example of an expression is 1 + 1. In that, Ruby can evaluate that expression and it will result to 2. The plus sign (+) is one of many operators in Ruby.

You can assign expression to a variable. The result of the expression will be stored on the variable instead of the expression itself. For example:

```
irb(main):001:0> a = 1 + 1
=> 2
```

If you check the value of a by inputting a into the shell, it will return 2 not 1 + 1.

As mentioned a while ago, expressions can also contain variables. If you assign a simple or complex expression with a variable to another variable, Ruby will handle all the evaluation. For example:

```
irb(main):001:0> a = 2
=> 2
irb(main):002:0> b = 4
=> 4
irb(main):003:0> c = a + b + 6
=> 12
```

Operators

Operators are symbols or keywords that command the computer to perform operations or evaluations. Ruby's operators are not limited to performing arithmetic operations alone. The following are the operators you can use in Ruby:

Arithmetic Operators

Arithmetic operators allow Ruby to evaluate simple Math expressions. They are: + for addition, - for subtraction, * for multiplication, / for division, % for modulus, and ** for exponent.

Division in Ruby works differently. If you are dividing integers, you will get an integer quotient. If the quotient should have a fractional component or decimal on it, they will be removed. For example:

```
irb(main):001:0> 5 / 2
=> 2
```

If you want to get an accurate quotient with a fractional component, you must perform division with fractional components For example:

```
irb(main):001:0> 5.0 / 2
=> 2.5
```

For those who are unfamiliar with modulus: modulus performs regular division and returns the remainder instead of the quotient. For example:

```
irb(main):001:0> 5 % 2
=> 1
```

Comparison Operators

Ruby can compare numbers, too, with the help of comparison operators. Comparison operations provide two results only: true or false. For example:

```
irb(main):001:0> 1 > 2
=> false
```

The value 1 is less than 2, but not greater than; therefore, Ruby evaluated that the expression is false.

Other comparison operators that you can use in Ruby are: == for has equal value, != for does not have equal value, > for greater than, < for less than, >= for greater than or equal, and <= for less than or equal. There four other comparison operators (===, <=>, .eql?, and .equal?) in Ruby, but you do not need them for now.

Assignment Operators

Assignment operators are used to assign value to operators, properties, and other entities in Ruby. You have already encountered the most used assignment operator, which is the equal sign (=). There are other assignment operators other than that, which are simple combination of the assignment operator (=) and arithmetic operators.

They are += for add and assign, -= for subtract and assign, *= for multiply and assign, /= for divide and assign, % for modulus and assign, and ** for raise and assign.

All of them perform the arithmetic operation and the values they use are the value of the entity on their left and the expression on their right first before assigning the result of the operation to the entity on its left. It might seem confusing, so here is an example:

```
irb(main):001:0> a = 1
```

```
=> 1
irb(main):002:0> a += 2
=> 3
```

In the example, variable a was given a value of 1. On the next statement, the add and assign operator was used. After the operation, a's value became 3 because a + 2 = 3. That can also be achieved by doing this:

```
irb(main):001:0> a = 1
=> 1
irb(main):002:0> a = a + 2
=> 3
```

If the value to the right of these operators is an expression that contain multiple values and operators, it will be evaluated first before the assignment operators perform their operations. For example:

```
irb(main):001:0> a = 1
=> 1
irb(main):002:0> a += 3 * 2
=> 7
```

The expression 3 * 2 was evaluated first, which resulted to 6. Then six was added to variable a that had a value of 1, which resulted to 7. And that value value was assigned to variable a.

Other Operators
As you advance your Ruby programming skills, you will encounter more operators. And they are:

- Logical Operator: and, or, &&, ||, !, not
- Defined Operator: defined?

- Reference Operators: ., ::

Chapter 5: Conditional Statements

Conditional statements allow programs to think and perform commands that are more intricate. Almost all programming languages offer conditional statements; Ruby shares the same conditional statements convention.

Using conditional statements will allow your program to perform specific tasks if the program, computer, or user meets certain conditions. You can use as many conditional statements as you want. The more conditional statements that you have, the more complex your program becomes.

With conditional statements, you will gain full control on how your program will work. You can create situations wherein some code block will be executed if they are truly needed and some code block will be ignored since they are not required to run yet.

By the way, be careful when it comes to mentioning 'block of code' in Ruby. Other Ruby programmers might misinterpret you. Blocks do have meaning in Ruby. Although it practically means the same as code block, confusion may arise. Anyway, blocks will not be discussed in this book.

Despite conditional statements can make your program more complex, conditional statements by themselves are simple. They cannot process any complicated conditions and it is up to the programmer on how the program can check and process conditions that are out of the basic conditional statement's scope.

Conditional statements operate in a simple manner. You need to place the conditional statement keyword, place your condition/s (or conditional), and the lines of codes that you want to execute in case that your condition gets satisfied.

These conditions only are answered with two options — True or False. If the condition is satisfied, the program will return a True value; if the condition is not satisfied, the program will return a False value.

If the conditional statement receives a True value, then it will process the lines of code written after the conditional statement. If the conditional statement receives a False value, then the lines of codes will be skipped and the program will move to the next statement. Though, some conditional constructs behave differently.

Puts, Print, and Gets

Before you go any further, you need to learn three of the most used basic commands or keywords when making simple programs in Ruby.

First, puts and print. Puts and print go hand in hand in Ruby. The main function of the two is to print strings or data on your program's console. However, the two prints data and strings differently.

To print something using those commands, you must follow this syntax:

```
irb(main):029:0> puts "insert text here"
insert text here
=> nil
irb(main):030:0> puts 1
1
=> nil
irb(main):031:0>   print   "You   can   print
numbers directly without using quotes."
You can print numbers directly without using
quotes.=> nil
<he other hand, you can print the content of
a variable just like below."
=> "On the other hand, you can print the
content of a variable just like below."
```

```
irb(main):033:0> puts $x
On the other hand, you can print the content
of a variable just like below.
=> nil
<you are printing strings, make sure that
you enclose them inside quotes. "
If you are printing strings, make sure that
you enclose them inside quotes. => n
il
<re are other tricks you can do with strings
and these two keywords."
There are other tricks you can do with
strings and these two keywords.=> nil
<variables inside the quotation marks using
the pounds sign"
Such as printing the value of variables
inside the quotation marks using the pou
nds sign
=> nil
irb(main):037:0> print "below is an example"
below is an example=> nil
irb(main):038:0> $y = "This is the string
inside variable y."
=> "This is the string inside variable y."
<t the content of the variable y after the
period. #$y "
Print the content of the variable y after
the period. This is the string inside
variable y.
=> nil
irb(main):040:0>
```

When you use puts, Ruby will create a line break after the line. On the other hand, print will not add any line break thus it is easier to print continuous text with it. Below is a comparison between the two:

```
irb(main):002:0> puts "this line will have a
line break after it"
this line will have a line break after it
=> nil
irb(main):003:0> print "while this one will
continue without a line break "
while this one will continue without a line
break => nil
irb(main):004:0>
```

On the other hand, the keyword gets is used to retrieve input from the user. When the gets keyword is processed, the program will pause and a cursor will wait for the user to input anything on the program. It will only accept inputs from the keyboard. To get out of gets or to submit the text that was typed, the user must press the Enter key.

If, Elsif, and Else Conditional Statements

One of the most basic structures of conditional statements is the if else (or if then else elseif) conditional statement. Below is an example of an if then else condition:

```
irb(main):233:0> x = 10
=> 10
irb(main):234:0> if x > 5
irb(main):235:1> puts "do some commands in
here "
irb(main):236:1> print "The if statement
checks if the value of variable x "
irb(main):237:1> print "is more than 5 "
irb(main):238:1> print "if variable xs value
is more than 5 "
irb(main):239:1> print "then this command
block will be processed. "
```

```
irb(main):240:1>  print  "and  you  will  see
these messages on your program "
irb(main):241:1> else
irb(main):242:1* print "however, if variable
xs value is not more than 5 "
irb(main):243:1>  print  "or  its  value  is
equal or less than 5 "
< statement block below the if statement
will not be executed "
<tead, the program will execute the command
block under else "
irb(main):246:1> print "which is this block.
"
irb(main):247:1> end
do some commands in here
The if statement checks if the value of
variable x is more than 5 if variable xs
value is more than 5 then this command block
will be processed. and you will see these
messages on your program => nil
irb(main):248:0>
```

Below is the syntax for the if and else conditional statements:

```
if <condition>
    <block  of  code  to  be  executed  if
condition returns True>
else
    <block  of  code  to  be  executed  if
condition returns False>
end
```

In the example, your program will check the variable x if it meets the condition set by the comparison operator > (greater than). If the value of x is greater, the if construct will receive the value of true, which will execute the code block below it.

The else construct behaves a bit different. In case that the if construct before the else construct returns False, the code block beneath the else construct will be executed. Alternatively, if the if statement receives True, then the code block beneath the else statement will be ignored.

Simply put, any code block placed below the if construct will be executed if the condition returns True, and any code block placed below the else construct will be executed if the condition returns False.

Aside from if and else, you can use elsif to add more complex conditions to your programs. Elsif is a combination of else and if. In other programming languages, they might be encoded as else if, elseif, and elif. Like if, elsif should have conditions, too. And like else, elsif will be processed in case the previous if statement returns False.

For example:

```
irb(main):262:0> if x > 10
irb(main):263:1> puts "The value of variable
x is more than 10."
irb(main):264:1> elsif x > 5
<value of variable x is less than 10 but
more than 5."
irb(main):266:1> else
irb(main):267:1* puts "The value of variable
x is less than 5."
irb(main):268:1> end
The value of variable x is less than 10 but
more than 5.
=> nil
irb(main):269:0> x
=> 10
irb(main):270:0>
```

You can add a lot of elsif in your code. However, be always mindful of the logic that you will apply to your code. It is essential that you avoid redundancy and too much unneeded complexity. For example:

```
irb(main):270:0> if x > 10
irb(main):271:1> puts "The value of variable
x is more than 10."
irb(main):272:1> elsif  x > 12
irb(main):273:1> puts "The value of variable
x is more than 12."
irb(main):274:1> else
irb(main):275:1* puts "The value of variable
x is less than 10 and 12."
irb(main):276:1> end
The value of variable x is less than 10 and
12.
=> nil
irb(main):277:0> x
=> 10
irb(main):278:0>
```

As you can see if ever the value of variable x will be more than 10, the if condition will return True. If that happens, the elsif and else codes will be ignored. Unfortunately, the elsif's condition is set to x > 12. All numbers more than 12 are more than 10. And that means that even before the program gets to the elsif line, the if will returns True and the program will never get to execute the code block for the elsif.

Unless and Else Conditional Statements

There will be times that you would want to create a conditional block wherein instead of your code block executing if the conditional you placed is True, it will execute when it receives False. You can do that by using the unless conditional statement. With unless, you can make a code block run if the condition is not satisfied. For example:

```
irb(main):278:0> unless x > 10
```

```
irb(main):279:1>  puts  "The  variable  x  is
less than 10."
irb(main):280:1> else
irb(main):281:1*  puts  "The  variable  x  is
more than 10."
irb(main):282:1> end
The variable x is less than 10.
=> nil
irb(main):283:0> x
=> 10
irb(main):284:0>
```

If ever the value of variable x is less than 10, the code block below the unless construct will be executed. On the other hand, the else construct works a bit different here. If else is placed below unless, the else code block will run if the unless conditional returns True. To prevent confusion, think of else as a construct that will run if the previous condition and its block did not process or is satisfied.

The unless follows the same syntax as if, elsif, and else:

```
unless <condition>
    <some  code  to  run  if  condition  returns
False>
else
    <some  code  to  run  if  condition  returns
True>
end
```

Case and When Conditional Statement

Instead of using a lot of elsif's in your program, you can make a more efficient way of placing multiple conditions. However, it only checks one expression and/or variable at a time. Nevertheless, it can become handy.

For example, if you want to create three conditions for variable x, you can do it this way:

```
irb(main):284:0> case x
irb(main):285:1> when 10
irb(main):286:1> puts "The variable xs value
is equal to 10."
irb(main):287:1> when 11
irb(main):288:1> puts "The variable xs value
is equal to 11."
irb(main):289:1> else
irb(main):290:1* puts "The variable xs value
is not 11 nor 10."
irb(main):291:1> end
The variable xs value is equal to 10.
=> nil
irb(main):292:0> x
=> 10
irb(main):293:0>
```

In the example, the first line says that the program will check on the value of variable x on the following conditional statements. After that, the next line serves as a condition and it translates to if variable x's value is 10, then execute the code. The same happens to the next lines. And when no code blocks were triggers, the code in the else block will run.

That example is equivalent to the one below if you use if and elsif instead:

```
irb(main):293:0> if x == 10
irb(main):294:1> puts "The variable xs value
is equal to 10."
irb(main):295:1> elsif x == 11
irb(main):296:1> puts "The variable xs value
is equal to 11."
irb(main):297:1> else
irb(main):298:1* puts "The variable xs value
is not 11 nor 10."
```

```
irb(main):299:1> end
The variable xs value is equal to 10.
=> nil
irb(main):300:0> x
=> 10
irb(main):301:0>
```

In small-scale projects, the difference between using if and case is marginally small. But if you will need to create intricate conditions on a value or expression, case and when will make your life easier and code cleaner and simpler.

To make you remember how to use it, below is the syntax for case and when:

```
case <variable or expression>
when <value>
    <some code>
when <value>
    <some code>
else
    <some code>
end
```

Conditional Modifiers

Sometimes, you will want to create one simple check to execute one statement. If you write one using the typical syntax of conditional statements, it seems too lengthy. Fortunately, you can shorten some conditional statements using modifiers. You can do that with if and unless. Below is an example of using the conventional conditional statement for if and unless.

```
irb(main):301:0> if x == 1
irb(main):302:1> puts "Variable xs value is
1. "
irb(main):303:1> end
```

41

```
=> nil
irb(main):304:0> if x < 15
irb(main):305:1> puts "Variable xs value is
more than 15. "
irb(main):306:1> end
Variable xs value is more than 15.
=> nil
irb(main):307:0> x
=> 10
irb(main):308:0>
```

By using conditional modifiers, you can shorten those codes into one statement. Below is a shorter version of the example above:

```
irb(main):308:0> puts "Variable xs value is
1. " if x == 1
=> nil
irb(main):309:0> puts "Variable xs value is
more than 15. " unless x < 15
=> nil
irb(main):310:0> x
=> 10
irb(main):311:0>
```

Chapter 6: Loops

In the previous chapter, you have learned how to control the flow of your program using conditional statements. Conditional statements allow you to make your program perform complex functions.

The next thing that you should learn is loops. Loops can allow you to execute a statement or block of code repeatedly depending on the number of loops you set or until a condition gets satisfied.

While Do Loop

Loops can help you reduce the redundancy of your statements. And they effectively simplify and clean your source code. For example, if you want to execute a statement that prints the numbers 1 to 5, you might code it like this:

```
irb(main):145:0> puts 1
1
=> nil
irb(main):146:0> puts 2
2
=> nil
irb(main):147:0> puts 3
3
=> nil
irb(main):148:0> puts 4
4
=> nil
irb(main):149:0> puts 5
5
=> nil
irb(main):150:0>
```

The example does achieve the goal of letting your program print the numbers 1, 2, 3, 4, and 5. However, it can be improved by using a loop. Below is an example of using a loop that also prints the numbers 1, 2, 3, 4, and 5.

```
irb(main):141:0>      while      $counter      <
$numberofloops do
irb(main):142:1* $counter += 1
irb(main):143:1> puts $counter
irb(main):144:1> end
1
2
3
4
5
=> nil
irb(main):145:0>
```

There are numerous loop methods that you can choose from in Ruby. The previous example used the while loop statement. If you convert the example code above to human language, it means:

- Set $counter variable to 0

- Set $numberofloops variable to 5

- While $counter variable is less than $numberofloops variable add 1 to the $counter variable and print its value

- If $counter variable is already more than the $numberofloops variable, end the loop

Of course, it might appear that the loop code in the example is much longer and a bit tedious than the example done without the loop. However, in large scale projects or even medium ones where you will need to repeat more than two or more statements repeatedly, using loops is much more efficient.

On the other hand, sound logic is again important in setting up conditions in loops. Two primary issues might happen if you set a problematic condition to your loop. First, the loop might not work; second, the loop might loop for eternity or indefinitely.

The first problem is harmless. However, the second one can be a pain. A loop that will run indefinitely will make your program unable to progress to the next line of code. In addition, a never-ending loop will take up all of your computer's resources. In a low end computer, that kind of loop will make the computer hang or unresponsive. In a high end computer, it will provide significant performance degradation or slowing down.

For referencing purposes, the syntax for the while do loop is:

```
while <condition> do
    <statements to be executed>
    <condition altering statement>
end
```

It is common that most while loops use integers to limit or determine the number of loops the program will do. A variable is used a counter and another variable or value is used to determine the max number of loops.

In the while do example, the $counter variable was used to count the number of times the loop has repeated. To make that variable act as a counter of some sort, the variable is given an increment of 1 every loop.

To limit the number of loops, the example used the variable $numberofloops. It was set to 5 in order to limit the loop to repeat 5 times. Then a conditional was placed ($counter > $numberofloops).

For every time the loop will repeat, the condition will be checked. If the condition returns True, the loop will repeat. Once the condition returns False, it will end the loop and move to the next statement after the end keyword. In the case of the example, once the $counter variable reaches 5 after being incremented 5 times, the loop stopped.

While Modifier

The while modifier has a different syntax and different method of looping. Unlike the regular while do loop, the while modifier checks the conditional statement after the code block within it is executed. Below is the syntax for the while modifier:

```
begin
    <statements to be executed>
end while <condition for loop>
```

Below is the previous example that uses the while modifier loop:

```
irb(main):135:0> begin
irb(main):136:1* $counter += 1
irb(main):137:1> puts $counter
irb(main):138:1>   end   while   $counter   <
$numberofloops
1
2
3
4
5
=> nil
irb(main):139:0>
```

Until Do Loop

The until do loop is a reversed version of the while do loop. Instead of looping when the condition returns True, it will loop when the condition returns False and it will stop when the condition returns True.

You can interchange the until do and while do depending on your coding style. But always take note that you need to change the way you want the loop to stop. Some programmers prefer to use only one of the two for the sake of uniformity in code and familiarity of loops.

In some programming languages, the until loop does not exist. On the other hand, some who are too meticulous prefer one loop over the other due to performance. Some loops work faster than others; however, the difference is usually marginally small and can be ignored if you are working on a small project.

Anyway, below is the 1 – 5 counter example that uses the until loop.

```
irb(main):104:0> $counter = 1
=> 1
irb(main):105:0> $numberofloops = 5
=> 5
irb(main):106:0>      until      $counter    >
$numberofloops do
irb(main):107:1* puts $counter
irb(main):108:1> $counter += 1
irb(main):109:1> end
1
2
3
4
5
=> nil
irb(main):110:0>
```

As you can see, the example is similar to the while do loop version. The main difference is the condition that was placed on the loop. Technically, since you are aiming for the condition to return False in order to loop, the condition or the comparison operator was just reversed.

Until Modifier

Until also has a modifier version. It is almost the same as the while modifier. And the only difference is that the loop will work if it receives a value of False. Below is the syntax for the until modifier:

```
begin
    <statements to be executed>
end until <condition for loop>
```

And below is the 1 – 5 counter processed using the until modifier:

```
irb(main):098:0> $counter = 1
=> 1
irb(main):099:0> $numberofloops = 5
=> 5
irb(main):100:0> begin
irb(main):101:1* puts $counter
irb(main):102:1> $counter += 1
irb(main):103:1>   end   while   $counter   >
$numberofloops
1
=> nil
irb(main):104:0>
```

For In Loop

In terms of popularity, the for loop has been contending with the while do loop. Both are usually present in programming languages. And it is commonly up to the programmer's preferences on which one he will use in his programs. Though, both have exclusive use in specific situations.

However, unlike while do loop, for loop has a built in counter of sort. Also, for loop cannot accept conditions. But you can easily specify the number of times you want it to loop on the get go. For example:

```
irb(main):095:0> for $counter in 1..5
irb(main):096:1> puts $counter
irb(main):097:1> end
1
2
3
4
5
=> 1..5
irb(main):098:0>
```
The for loop automatically creates a variable to be used as a counter, add a starting value to it, increment it by 1 every loop, and if reaches the max number (or last number in the range) its loop will stop.

The syntax for the for loop is below:

```
for <variable to be used as a counter> in
<starting value> .. <ending value>
    <code block to be executed>
End
```

Take note that the variable that you use as a counter is only useable as a means to count the number of loops the for loop has done or the current number it is on the range. Even if you try to change the value of the $counter within your block of code, the for in statement will revert the number back to the number it is on the range. For example:

```
irb(main):092:0> for $counter in 1..5
irb(main):093:1> puts $counter
irb(main):094:1> end
```

```
1
2
3
4
5
=> 1..5
irb(main):095:0>
```

If you run the example above, the variable $counter will be still printed with numbers since the for loop will reassign the range value to it. Nevertheless, it does not mean that the value will not be changed. For example:

```
for $counter in 1..5
    $counter = "Hello"
    puts $counter
end
```

In that example, the for loop will print five Hello's instead.

Each Do Loop

The each do loop is relatively similar to the for in loop. It uses a range of integer numbers to limit the number of loops it does. However, it does not use any variable to act as a counter. So, in case that you will need a counter that you can use in your code block, you must manually place a statement that will provide increments on it.

```
$counter = 0
(1..5).each do
$counter += 1
    puts $counter
end
The syntax for the each do loop is below:
(<start number>..<end number>).each do
    <block of code to be executed>
end
```

As mentioned before, both for and while (and until) can be used in some specific situations. Below is an example of a number guessing game:

```
$number = 0
puts "Guess the number"
puts "Type only numbers"
puts "Including letters, signs, symbols, or
blanks on your guess will crash this
program"
puts "Press enter to submit your guess"
puts "The program will loop until you guess
the correct number"
while Integer($number) != 5 do
$number = gets.chomp
puts "Congratulations! You have guessed the
right number! This program will close now!"
if Integer($number) == 5
end
```

If you want to use the until loop, then you can try this instead:

```
$number = 0
puts "Guess the number"
puts "Type only numbers"
puts "Including letters, signs, symbols, or
blanks on your guess will crash this
program"
puts "Press enter to submit your guess"
puts "The program will loop until you guess
the correct number"
until Integer($number) == 5 do
$number = gets.chomp
puts "Congratulations! You have guessed the
right number! This program will close now!"
if Integer($number) == 5
end
```

Break Statement

Aside from making the condition in the loop get a different result, you can use the break statement to get out of the loop. The break statement can be used to abruptly stop the loop depending on its location or how it will be placed.

Once your program sees a break statement in the open, it will immediately skip to the end statement and proceed on executing the statements outside the loop. Of course, you do not want to just place a break in the open since it will prevent your loop from repeating. Due to that, it is common that break statements are used in conjunction with conditional statements.

Conditional statements in addition to break can allow you to have full control of your loop and add complexity to your program. For example, below is guess a number program:

```
irb(main):071:0> $number = 0
=> 0
irb(main):072:0> $maxtries = 10
=> 10
irb(main):073:0> puts "Guess the number"
Guess the number
=> nil
irb(main):074:0> puts "Type only numbers"
Type only numbers
=> nil
<ols, or blanks on your guess will crash
this program"
Including letters, signs, symbols, or blanks
on your guess will crash this progr
am
=> nil
irb(main):076:0> puts "Press enter to submit
your guess"
Press enter to submit your guess
```

```
=> nil
<program  will  only  give  you  #$maxtries
attempts to guess"
The  program  will  only  give  you  10  attempts
to guess
=> nil
irb(main):078:0>    puts    "After    #$maxtries
attempts, the program will close"
After 10 attempts, the program will close
=> nil
<iding  a  correct  guess  will  also  terminate
the program"
Providing   a   correct   guess   will   also
terminate the program
=> nil
irb(main):080:0>
irb(main):081:0*       for       $counter       in
(1..$maxtries)
irb(main):082:1> puts "You  have  #$maxtries
remaining guess(es)!"
irb(main):083:1> $number = gets.chomp
irb(main):084:1> $maxtries -= 1
irb(main):085:1> if Integer($number) == 5
<sed  the  right  number!  This  program  will
close now!"
irb(main):087:2> break
irb(main):088:2> end
irb(main):089:1> puts "Wrong!" if $maxtries
!= 0
irb(main):090:1> puts "Tough luck, bro!" if
$maxtries == 0
irb(main):091:1> end
You have 10 remaining guess(es)!
1
Wrong!
You have 9 remaining guess(es)!
2
Wrong!
You have 8 remaining guess(es)!
3
```

```
Wrong!
You have 7 remaining guess(es)!
5
Congratulations! You have guessed the right
number! This program will close now!

=> nil
irb(main):092:0>
```

In the example, if ever the player was able to guess the right number, the loop will break and the puts statements after the if block will be skipped.

Next Statement

Aside from immediately stopping a loop, you can also skip one or more repetitions of your code block. And you can do that with the next statement. An executed next statement will make the loop ignore any statements after it and skip immediately to the conditional check of the loop. For example:

```
irb(main):067:0> for $counter in 1..5
irb(main):068:1> next if $counter < 3
irb(main):069:1> puts $counter
irb(main):070:1> end
3
4
5
=> 1..5
irb(main):071:0>
```

Redo Statement

Another loop control statement that you can use is redo. The redo statement will make your loop repeat once again. However, instead of just repeating, the loop will skip the conditional check. For example:

```
$counter = 1
$numberofloops = 5
until $counter > $numberofloops do
    puts $counter
    $counter += 1
retry if $counter < 5
end
```

In the example, the code will become an infinite loop. Since the redo statement will be processed every time the loop is processed and the conditional is not checked, there will be no way that the loop will stop. Even if the $counter reaches a value more than the value of $numberofloops, the loop will continue since the conditional of the loop is ignored.

Chapter 7: Methods

In Ruby, you can create a block of code that you can call anytime. And that is to create or define methods. Unlike conditional statements that has a block of code, methods do not need the program to satisfy a condition before it runs. Instead, you need to call it. You can say that some of the keywords in Ruby are built-in methods of Ruby. A good example of that is the gets keyword.

Whenever the program sees a gets keyword in your source code, it will perform multiple statements or instructions in order for its purpose to work — in this case, to pause the program, wait for user input, and take the characters that was typed and submitted. That is how methods work, too. Below is an example of how to define or create a method in Ruby.

```
irb(main):001:0> def this_is_a_method ()
irb(main):002:1> puts "Statement 1"
irb(main):003:1> puts "Statement 2"
irb(main):004:1> puts "Statement 3"
irb(main):005:1> end
=> :this_is_a_method
irb(main):006:0>
```

In case you want to create a method similar to gets, you might want to do it this way:

```
irb(main):001:0> def your_own_gets ()
irb(main):002:1>    <statements    to    pause
program>
irb(main):003:1> <statements to require user
input>
irb(main):004:1> <statements  to  store  data
that was submitted>
```

```
irb(main):005:1>    <statements    to    resume
program flow>
irb(main):006:1> end
=> :your_own)gets
irb(main):007:0>
```

Anyway, once you entered the previous example on your source code, your program will have a 'keyword' or method named this_is_a_method. You can invoke or call this method by just typing it out and placing it as a standalone statement — just like how you would do if you want to use gets. For example:

```
irb(main):000:0> this_is_a_method
Statement 1
Statement 2
Statement 3
=> nil
irb(main):001:0>
```

Once a method was called or invoked, all the statements within it will be processed. That is how simple methods work.

Method Parameters

How about if you want to create a method like puts or print that can accept some values and perform some functions on those values? Well, in that case, you will need to place some parameters on your method.

Parameters are temporary variables that can take arguments or data when the method is invoked. These temporary variables can be used within the statements within the method's code block. For example, create your own puts method.

```
irb(main):001:0> def myputs (texttoprint)
irb(main):002:1>   puts texttoprint
```

```
irb(main):003:1> end
=> :myputs
irb(main):004:0>
```

After putting that in your program, try using the method myputs like puts. For example:

```
irb(main):000:0> myputs "Test"
Test
=> nil
irb(main):001:0>
```

As you can see, the parameter took the argument that has the value of "Test", the puts statement took its value, and printed it.

When creating methods, you are not limited to use one parameter alone. The example below will use two parameters:

```
irb(main):001:0> def addnumbers (add1, add2)
irb(main):002:1> sum = add1 + add2
irb(main):003:1> puts sum
irb(main):004:1> end
=> :addnumbers
irb(main):005:0>
```

The method will allow you to add two numbers. Once you call it, you will also need to give it two arguments that are separated with a comma. For example:

```
irb(main):000:0> addnumbers 1, 2
3
=> nil
irb(main):001:0>
```

Chapter 8: Object Oriented Programming

In the previous chapters, you have learned the basics of Ruby programming. Those chapters also serve as your introduction to computer programming since most programming languages follow the same concepts and have similar entities in them. In this chapter, you will learn why some programmers love Ruby.

Ruby is an Object Oriented Programming (OOP) language. Object oriented programming makes use of objects and classes. Those objects and classes can be reused which in turn makes it easier to code programs that require multiple instances of values that are related to each other.

Programming methods can be categorized into two: Procedural and Object Oriented. If you have experienced basic programming before, you mostly have experienced procedural instead of object oriented.

In procedural, your program's code revolves around actions. For example, you have a program that prints what a user will input. It is probable that your program's structure will be as simple as take user input, assign the input to a variable, and then print the content of the variable. As you can see, procedural is a straightforward forward method.

Classes and Objects

Classes are like templates for objects. For example, a Fender Telecaster and a Gibson Les Paul are objects and they are under the electric guitar class.

In programming, you can call those guitars as instances of the class of objects named electric guitars. Each object has its own properties or characteristics.

Objects under the same class have same properties, but the value of those properties may differ or be the same per object. For example, think that an electric guitar's properties are: brand, number of strings, and number of guitar pickups.

Aside from that, each object has its own functions or things that it can do. When it comes to guitars, you can strum all the strings or you can just pick on one string.

If you convert that to Ruby code, that will appear as:

```
irb(main):001:0> class ElectricGuitar
irb(main):002:1> def initialize
irb(main):003:2>
irb(main):003:2> @brand = Local
irb(main):004:2>
irb(main):004:2> @strings = 6
irb(main):005:2>
irb(main):005:2> @pickups = 3
irb(main):006:2> end
irb(main):007:1> def strum
irb(main):008:2>
irb(main):008:2> #Insert statements to
execute when strum is called
irb(main):009:2* end
irb(main):010:1> def pick
irb(main):011:2>
irb(main):011:2> #Insert statements to
execute when strum is called
irb(main):012:2* end
irb(main):013:1>
```

Creating a Class

To create a class, you need to use the class keyword and an identifier. Class identifiers have the same syntax rules for constant identifiers. To end the creation of the class, you need to use the end keyword. For example:

```
irb(main):001:0> class Guitar
irb(main):002:1> end
=> nil
```

Creating an Object

Now, you have a class. It is time for you to create an object. To create one, all you need is to think of an identifier and assign the class name and the keyword new to it for it to become an object under a class. For example:

```
irb(main):001:0> fender = Guitar. new
=> #<Guitar:0x1234567>
```

Note: Do not forget to add a dot operator after the class name.

Unfortunately, the class Guitar does not contain anything in it. That object is still useless and cannot be used for anything. To make it useful, you need to add some methods and properties to it.

Methods

This is where it gets interesting. Methods allow your objects to have 'commands' of some sort. In case you want to have multiple lines of statements to be done, placing them under a class method is the best way to do that. To give your classes or objects methods, you will need to use the def (define) keyword. Below is an example:

```
irb(main):001:0> class Guitar
irb(main):002:1> def strum
irb(main):003:2> puts "Starts strumming. "
```

```
irb(main):004:2> puts "Strumming. "
irb(main):005:2> puts "Ends strumming. "
irb(main):006:2> end
irb(main):007:1> end
=> :strum
```

Now, create a new object under that class.

```
irb(main):008:0> gibson = Guitar. new
=> #<Guitar:0x1234567>
```

To use the method you have created, all you need is to invoke it using the object. For example:

```
irb(main):009:0> gibson.strum
Starts strumming.
Strumming.
Ends strumming.
=> nil
```

By using the dot operator, you were able to invoke the method inside the gibson object under the Guitar class. All the objects that will be under Guitar class will be able to use that method.

Conclusion

Thank you again for purchasing this book!

I hope this book was able to help you understand how coding in Ruby works.

The next step is to:

- Learn more about flow control tools in Ruby

- Study about the other operators discussed in this book

- Research on how variables inside classes and objects work

Finally, if you enjoyed this book, please take the time to share your thoughts and post a review on Amazon. We do our best to reach out to readers and provide the best value we can. Your positive review will help us achieve that. It'd be greatly appreciated!

Thank you and good luck!

Check Out My Other Books

Below you'll find some of my other popular books that are popular on Amazon and Kindle as well. Simply click on the links below to check them out. Alternatively, you can visit my author page on Amazon to see other work done by me.

C Programming Success in a Day

Python Programming Success in a Day

PHP Programming Professional Made Easy

HTML Professional Programming Made Easy

CSS Programming Professional Made Easy

Windows 8 Tips for Beginners

C Programming Professional Made Easy

JavaScript Programming Made Easy

Rails Programming Professional Made Easy

C ++ Programming Success in a Day

If the links do not work, for whatever reason, you can simply search for these titles on the Amazon website to find them.

www.ingramcontent.com/pod-product-compliance
Lightning Source LLC
Chambersburg PA
CBHW070942180526
45168CB00003B/1146